Peace

In the Midst of Pain

A Widow's Journal

by

Betsy Martin Brackbill

PEACE IN THE MIDST OF PAIN

A Widow's Journal

All Scripture quotations are taken from the *Holy Bible: New International Version NIV*, Copyright 1973, 1978, 1984 by International Bible Society. "My Jesus, as thou Wilt" by Benjamin Schmolk, 1716, translated by June Borthwick, 1854, music by Carl M. von Weber, 1821. "My Pilgrimage" by Isaac Martin, *Lancaster Mennonite Conference News*, 1982. "Be Still My Soul" by Katharina von Schlegel. "A Mighty Fortress Is Our God" by Martin Luther, 1529. *Lancaster New Era*, December 12, 1989. *Miami Herald*, December 12, 1989. *Intelligencer Journal*, December 18, 1989.

Portions of this story first appeared in *Shared Burdens: Stories of Caring Practices Among Mennonites*. Copyright by Good Books (www.goodbks.com). Used by permission. All rights reserved.

Library of Congress Number: 2002115321
International Standard Book Number: 1-930353-70-7

Printed by
Masthof Press
219 Mill Road
Morgantown, PA 19543-9516

Acknowledgements

Special thanks to....

- My children who urged me to put this journal into print. Without their encouragement it would never have gotten further than my closet.

- My sister, Ruth Ann Hollinger, for her encouragement, for typing the manuscript and offering her imput into presenting the book to publishers as well as the editing.

- My sister, Lillian Weber, for editing the journal.

- My husband, Paul Brackbill, for his support.

- My brother, Sam Weber, for the sunrise photo on the cover.

Granddaughter Lisa standing in front of the bus that Ike and Betsy took to Miami for shipping to Costa Rica.

Peace In the Midst of Pain

There are times in our lives when everything that is normal and taken for granted is suddenly snatched away and the unreal becomes reality. Although our minds, incapable of absorbing this sudden turn of events, loudly protest "this can't be happening to me," there it is.

It was December 9, 1989, when my husband Ike and I left our home in the small town of Leola, Pennsylvania, enroute to Miami, Florida. The sparkling snow lay over the landscape, covering shrubs and trees, creating a beauty that decried the danger of the slick streets we were traveling. We were riding in a used school bus which we planned to ship to Costa Rica for the church where our daughter, Dolores, and her husband attended and where our son-in-law was pastor.

I was reluctant to leave at this time because it was so close to Christmas with all the activity accompanying the holiday. But it had already taken four months to work through all the legalities of purchasing the bus and now that everything was finally completed, Ike was eager to have it delivered to its final destination. Besides, it would be more difficult to find a break from his job as dispatcher at an oil company later in the winter. So in spite of the precariousness of the weather and the inconvenient timing, we were on our way.

Although I knew my husband was a skillful, experienced driver, I sat tensely in the seat behind him silently praying for safety as I observed the cars that had slipped off the road. We crept cautiously along for miles until finally the icy roads were behind us. That night we crawled into bed exhausted, and so relieved that the danger was past. Never in our wildest imaginations could we have guessed what lay before us.

We arrived in Miami on Monday, December 11, and spent the day acquiring a bill of lading, performing the necessary inspections, and renting a car for our use after the bus was gone. The last detail was completed around 5:00 p.m.—too late to get the bus through customs. We'd have to wait until morning to have it shipped, so we decided to find a motel and have dinner. I was following the bus in the rented car. Since it was difficult staying together in the heavy traffic on Route 95, we headed for a nearby inn that we had spotted just off the freeway.

While I checked in at the front desk, Ike found a place to park the bus. We were both hungry since we hadn't taken time for lunch, so with our suitcases still in the car trunk, we crossed the street to a Chinese restaurant.

After our meal, we again crossed the street to the hotel, not realizing that we had strayed into a high drug and crime area of the city.

Darkness was approaching as we attempted to enter the gate to the fenced-in parking lot. We were surprised to find it locked, but knowing there was another entrance on the opposite side of the building, we headed toward it. Just as we turned the corner, two young black men stepped out in front of us and demanded my purse. I was carrying only a small amount of money in my purse but I also had in it the title and the documents we needed to ship the bus. We didn't want to lose them and Ike said, "No, don't take that."

I was about to offer them my cash, but before I could speak, one of them pulled out a small handgun and putting it to Ike's head, pulled the trigger.

I watched horrified as he fell to the ground. A scream pierced the air and although I wasn't conscious of having done it, I knew it was my own. I knelt to see if I could feel a heartbeat, but what I saw didn't give any hope that there would be one. Almost immediately people began to arrive on the scene.

Although I later learned that racial tension was acute in that area, a large black man came and placing his arm around me, gently tried to lead me away and shield me from that sight.

The police arrived and put me in one of their cars while they cordoned off the area. As the ambulance crew knelt over Ike trying to save his life, I sat in the police car praying desperately that God would let him live.

They left for the hospital with Ike, while two detectives took me to the homicide offices of the police department.

Shaking uncontrollably in shock, I answered their questions the best I could. The detective showed me a list of names on the office wall and informed me that these were all the people murdered in Miami that year. "If Ike dies, he will only be a statistic to them," I thought incredulously. How wrong I was!

I gave a deposition and looked through stacks of mug shots in an attempt to identify the men who had attacked us. The detectives did everything they could for me and helped me make phone calls to my family.

After about an hour the news came from the hospital that Ike was dead. I was too numb to cry. As I sat at the detective's desk stunned and in shock, he tried to think of the right words to say.

I listened while he vented his own frustration and anger that such a thing could happen to a man like my husband. He said he hoped that those men would be caught and given the death sentence. He asked if I would be alone now, or if there would be someone to support me during this time. I told him I had my faith in God, my family, and my church and I knew they would all be there for me. Yet I had no concept of the profundity of those words.

After three or four hours, Ike's sister, Mary Alice, who lived in Immokalee, Florida, came with her friend, Thelma, and her pastor and his wife. They stayed up all night to come and take me to Immokalee with them.

Before we left the police station, the detective drove to the hotel to get my suitcases out of our rental car. When he returned, he was holding the envelope which contained all the bus documents I thought were gone with my stolen purse.

He said he'd found them in the back seat of the car. I didn't know how they got there, but I knew that in spite of everything that had happened, God was most certainly still in control.

We arrived at Mary Alice's home early Tuesday morning. I spent most of the morning on the phone with calls to the funeral director, to the hospital giving them instructions to release Ike's body, and calls concerning the bus and the change in plans for shipping it that morning. Detectives and news reporters were calling and there were the calls to keep in touch with my four children. A Christian radio announcer in Miami phoned and said that since the news of Ike's murder was broadcast, they were being inundated with calls from people wanting to know what they could do to help. Another man introducing himself as a private Miami citizen, wanted me to know that people all over the city were praying for my family and me and that many churches were having special prayer for us.

Later in the afternoon, Mary Alice and I left for the airport to return home to Leola. The phone rang one last time as we were leaving the house. It was the detective with the news that two airlines had offered free flights home for me and to have Ike's body flown back to Pennsylvania.

When our plane landed in Philadelphia, two of my brothers-in-law met us at the airport. Ike's youngest sister, Naomi, had been struck and killed by a drunken driver only three years earlier. That such a violent tragedy could strike the family again so soon, left us stunned and in a state of disbelief. "What does God want from our family?" questioned Ike's brother.

After my return home I began keeping a journal. It was helpful to write down my struggles, thoughts, and feelings. I could go back and read again all the positive caring ways in which God had displayed his love for me through this experience. How easy it was to forget when nothing seemed right and I felt drowned in despair.

It is my prayer that as you read this journal and as you walk with me through my grief towards recovery, that it may strengthen your own faith in God and encourage you in whatever struggles or sorrows you may have.

———————

December 12, 1989

The others talked about their memories of Ike on the ride home from the airport. His brother Mark told about the time when as teenagers he and Ike accompanied by some young friends went to a restaurant for breakfast. Misreading the menu, Ike put them all into gales of laughter by ordering "pooched" eggs. Listening to their conversation, I tried to grasp the fact that he will only be a memory now.

We pulled into the driveway around midnight. Donna, Dawn and Loren were lying on the floor in the den. They came to the door and hugged me—except Loren. He stayed lying there and didn't say anything. He's always been quiet and reserved. I sat on the floor and put my arms around him. What will it be like for him now without a father?

We talked for a long time about what had happened. They told me about the three TV interviews they had given that day. I was thankful the reporters were gone before I arrived home.

Dawn brought the Bible and read to us about heaven. We tried to visualize their dad there with God. After we prayed, the children spread out on the floor of the family room so they could be close together.

December 13, 1989

The phone is ringing constantly—friends, family and more reporters wanting interviews. A policeman from Lancaster arrived with a portfolio of eyes, ears, noses, and hairlines to put together a composite drawing of our assailants. As I struggled to remember some identifiable characteristics of those two faces that had appeared and as quickly were gone, Dolores, Martin, and baby Derick walked in the door. The policeman waited

Dolores and Martin with son Derick.

patiently as we embraced and spent a few minutes together. Derick is so cute and such a delight. A dear little two-year-old distraction is just what I need. Ike was so proud of him when they visited in July but Derick will probably never remember his grandfather now.

Martin has been struggling with feeling responsible for Ike's death; if he hadn't asked us to deliver the bus to Miami the tragedy wouldn't have occurred. But Ike

Ike and Derick in July before Ike's death.

wanted to do it. He felt good about Dolores' and Martin's involvement in the Costa Rican church and was eager to make a
contribution in this way. I know God has some plan, some
reason for all of this and no one is to blame.

December 14, 1989

Martin took me into Lancaster to the police station. A
detective from Miami met us there with some mug shots of
suspects, but none of them looked familiar to me. He said they
had questioned about ten young men who were claiming
responsibility for Ike's death because of the extensive news
coverage. Bragging to their buddies that they had done it apparently gave them a sense of importance. I know for the good of
the public those responsible for the shooting should be
caught, but the thought of returning to Miami for a trial makes
me feel ill.

The detective told us the Dade County police have never
had a homicide like this one. He said that racial tension was a
very serious problem in that area. A Hispanic policeman was
responsible for the death of a black man and the incident
had sparked riots. The atmosphere was just beginning to
stabilize when Ike was shot. He was afraid the riots would
re-ignite since the incident again involved two races. But now,
he continued, the black community was calling the police
station wanting to help solve the case even though it involved
two of their own who had committed a crime against a white
man. Such things, he explained, never happen and it was
giving the police department a renewed confidence in
society.

Later in the day, Ike's parents, Titus and Edna Martin, his
sisters, Mary Alice and Betty, Pastor Randy, the children and I

met with the funeral director to plan the service. We decided to have it on Sunday. It seems such a long time away. I feel numb, as though I've been put into a deep freeze and I know I'm still in shock.

It would be easier to have the funeral before this numbness wears off, but Ike's nephew is to be married on Saturday and we felt it would be easier for the family to postpone the services until after the wedding. I regret that such a happy occasion must be clouded by this sad turn of events.

Pastor Randy has been very helpful and supportive. He called the news media and asked them to channel their requests through him to relieve us. They wanted my permission to set up their cameras in the church for the funeral, but I declined. I need some privacy at a time like this.

December 15, 1989

Together our family went to choose a casket. Ike wouldn't have approved of purchasing an expensive one, but we wanted it to be nice. The children joked and acted silly, their way of coping with it all.

The funeral director had previously told us he wouldn't be able to repair the damage to Ike's head well enough for a viewing. Today he said he could reconstruct it well enough for just the immediate family to view if we wished, but that it would be disfigured. I didn't want to see it again. I knew I must block from my mind the sight I saw at the shooting and I was afraid viewing his body would reinforce that image and make it more difficult. However, I wanted the children to make that decision for themselves. They all agreed they would rather not see their father in that condition and retain that memory. For that I was silently grateful.

When we returned home, Dawn began to have doubts about the wisdom of that decision. Living in New York and unable to come home frequently, she feared if she didn't view his body, she could not come to terms with his death. As we sat and talked, the phone rang and the voice on the other end of the line identified herself as a woman who had lost her husband twenty years ago at the hands of a robber.

Although she didn't know us, she felt compelled to call. She recalled at the time she wanted to view his body but wasn't given that option. Now, years, later she is thankful she hadn't and instead has good mental pictures to remember him by. Her call gave Dawn the assurance that her first reaction was the best. The Lord looks after us even in minor things; He'll surely take care of our major needs.

———————

The phone continues to ring. County Commissioner James Huber called to express his condolences and also a black minister from Miami who told me how badly the black Christian community feels that the men who took my husband's life were black. Another call came from a resident of the Miami guest house with an offer to take the bus to the port and see that it was shipped. The shipping company will transport the bus to Costa Rica at no charge, saving the church $1800.00. God is so good.

There is a constant stream of people coming and going, bringing food and flowers. I know I must eat, so I try to force something down. It all seems like a dreadful dream—I'll awaken and everything will be all right again.

This morning as I picked up Ike's Bible, it fell open to the notes he had left there from teaching the Sunday School class the week before. He had asked each one to think of an experience they had gone through when God was especially close to them and then to think of a way they could share it with others. It was as though the notes had been left there just for me. Ever since the first moment of this experience God has been so near, giving me strength and calmness in the most overwhelming way. I prayed that God will help me to be faithful in sharing any way He wants.

I have been able to fall into a deep sleep every night as soon as I go to bed, although I awaken early in the morning. But I get enough hours of sound sleep to wake feeling rested. Several people have told me they were praying during the night that I'd be able to sleep and the Lord has answered their prayers. "Thank you, Lord, for such loving caring friends."

Sunday, December 17

Today the funeral was held at the New Holland Mennonite Church. It wasn't the ordeal I expected it to be. Six hundred people came to pay their respects to Ike and offer comfort to us. The news reporters stayed at a distance, respecting my wishes.

The service was very meaningful. Pastor Randy challenged everyone to live their lives in service to God.

Ike was a good man, a good husband and father, but he was human and had faults as every other person. I didn't want him to be placed on a pedestal because of the way he died. Randy summed it up adeptly by saying, "Ike was an ordinary man with an extraordinary God." The congregation sang, "A Mighty Fortress is our God. The body they may kill; God's truth abideth still." The words of that old familiar hymn stood out in stark reality today. Surely God's truth does still stand.

After the graveside service, most of the people left quickly, eager to get into their warm cars and out of the frigid winter weather. As I stood by the grave I placed a single carnation on the casket. I knew this was a final good-bye and the tears flowed. But it was only a final good-bye on earth. I will see him again.

I waken three to four hours before the others each morning and spend that time alone with God. The verses in the Bible seem electrified with meaning for me. "Never will I leave you, never will I forsake you." Hebrews 13:5. "God is our refuge and strength, an ever present help in time of trouble." Psalm 46:1. How often I had read those verses, but never before have I experienced the depth of their meaning as I do now. It's as though God put them there just for me.

I have received many letters from residents of Miami. One man wrote,

> *I want you to know that our city is shocked and out-raged at what has happened to your family. We are praying for you. We are praying for ourselves as well.*

Another one said,

> *I cried when I heard the tragic story of you and Isaac. Please remember that many of us in Miami love you and lift up your spirit to our loving Father for strength. Please pray for us in Miami, until we are all united in heaven.*

Still another:

> *We want to express our sympathy to you and your family. Our church is located a few blocks from where*

this terrible incident occurred. As Southern Baptist missionaries we have been working in this area for several years, teaching boys and girls in Bible clubs. They are praying for you. Only our dear Lord can comfort, but we want you to know many Christians in Miami are remembering you in prayer.

One lady wrote,

I want to express my family's extreme sorrow over what happened to your father and husband here in Miami. This is a rough place but there are many good people here who are trying to help better the situation.

And a letter from a Miami minister:

Our hearts are grieved at the events which led to the tragic loss of your husband. My family knew of nothing else to do but pray for you and your family. We prayed that He would minister to you in your deep needs and hurts. Miami is also a community of loving Christians who share in your ache and pain.

I've received hundreds of cards and letters from people saying they are praying for me. Yes, I can feel the power of those prayers.

Last night I dreamed that the men who killed Ike were trying to break into our house. I awoke paralyzed with fear and the room seemed filled with evil. A verse came to me, "Resist the devil and he will flee from you." I did that and the air cleared. I felt calm and peaceful and went back to sleep. People often tell me how strong I have been through all of this. God reminded me very clearly last night where that strength comes from. I could never be foolish enough to think I have it within myself.

December 25, 1989

It's Christmas. This morning Loren went to the convenience store to buy some milk and two apparently drunk men ran into the car and smashed the side. I've never paid any attention to the upkeep of the cars or the insurance. Ike always took care of those things. But Ike isn't here. It would have been so easy to succumb to the depression closing in on me.

We all went to the Martin family gathering for dinner. It was so hard being there without Ike and it was difficult to keep the tears back. I couldn't wait to get home where I could have a good long cry in the privacy of my room. What a wonderful release there is in tears.

Dawn's boyfriend, Brian, is here with us for a few days. It helps to have the house full of people. I suppose it gives me less time to think troubling thoughts.

December 29, 1989

I needed to have the titles to our two cars changed from Ike's name; one into Loren's and one into mine. Everyone has been so helpful. Charlie, our lawyer, has taken care of all my legal work and does it without charge.

I cleaned out Ike's closet and drawers, wanting to give the children his possessions before Dolores leaves for Costa Rica and Dawn for New York. He had a junk drawer full of old guitar books, church leadership records, and notes from classes he had taken. He liked to save things for which I could see no earthly purpose in keeping, but I restrained my clearing out tendencies as long as it could be contained in this allotted space.

As I sorted through the papers, I found a workbook we'd done years ago with the youth in our Bible studies during the six years we had served as youth advisors at church. One of the exercises was to fill out your own obituary. Two of the questions were, "What would you like to be doing when you die and what would you like people to say about you at your funeral?" Ike wrote that he would like to be acting as a good Samaritan to someone when he dies and he would like people to say he tried to serve God and others. He never would have believed that his death notice would be on the front page headlines of the two local newspapers. The first paragraph of the *Lancaster New Era* article stated, "A Leola man described as good, gentle and kind who was dedicated to helping others was killed Monday night in Miami where he had gone to arrange delivery of a bus to his daughter's church in Costa Rica."

In the coverage of his funeral, the headlines were, "As Martin is laid to rest, memory of charity lives." The *Miami Herald* headlines read, "Visitor on church mission slain in Miami."

Both Lancaster and Miami radio and TV news channels covered the story extensively. A spokesman for WSVN-TV said the shooting was the lead story throughout the day because it was an outrageous crime. People in Miami are upset that an innocent man coming down to do a good deed was brutally murdered on the streets. God certainly pulled out all the stops when He granted Ike's wishes. He does work in mysterious ways. I wonder what it all means. Finally I was able to read those news articles and watch the TV coverage the children had taped. I couldn't bear to look at them before.

Three people had premonitions that something tragic was going to happen when they learned we were going to Florida. One was upset for not having told us; that maybe Ike's death could have been prevented. Others said Ike was such a gentle man; it's not right that he should die like that. It's easy to adopt an "if only"—"what if" mode of thinking at times like this. But I feel confident that this was God's will and the only way we will all find peace is to accept the fact that God has every detail of our lives in His plan and under His control. I do believe that "In all things God works for good to those who love Him." Romans 8:28.

Even though we don't know the reasons for the events in our lives, God is there for us, comforting us and sending others to hold us until we're able to stand again. My life seemed completely out of control these past weeks, but it has forced me to rely entirely on Him and in doing so I have found peace in the midst of pain and grief. It has helped me realize how much I need others and helped me release my proud self sufficiency. Little irritations and disagreements are forgotten and all our masks are dropped when we face such traumatic situations; situations that call forth such intense emotions. Concerns about making a good impression in our interactions with each other don't exist at times like this and I find we are able to relate to one another on a deeply genuine level. That in turn helps to generate a real love and appreciation for each other. Suffering and death make us stop and listen to what God has to say. I've heard Him say "I love you" through His word and through His people.

January 2, 1990

"Lord, I don't want to be a widow. I want Ike back." Today I found his old work shoes in the garage which he used for mowing the lawn and working on the cars. They were worn and dirty and I went to throw them away. Suddenly the reality and the finality of his death hit me with a surge of pain. It was like throwing a part of myself away. "Lord, please help me trust you to bring me through this."

January 8, 1990

I'm still getting visitors every day and people often take me out to eat. Everyone is so kind. I know this isn't a good time with people dropping by so frequently, but I've begun tearing down the old paper in the kitchen to re-paper the walls. Somehow it brings a little normalcy to my life.

I had a visit from a couple whose son was killed in an accident a few weeks before Ike was shot. They brought a basket of fruit explaining that the same basket had been given to them from someone who had also lost a loved one. They requested that after the fruit was gone, I would refill it and pass it on to another grieving person.

I immediately thought of a young neighbor who had recently lost her husband in an accident. What an interesting way to reach out to another hurting person and show you understand and care. While death separates, it also firmly bonds those who are left behind.

January 15, 1990

Another day . . . what a beautiful sunrise. "Lord, will there be a sunrise for me, a new beginning, a new day in my life?"

Last night I met with our bishop, James, and the rest of the leadership team from church. We met to help a couple find a way to work through the problems in their marriage. I didn't want to go without Ike but the others urged me to come and I know I need to force myself to get back into my old activities. After the meeting James asked if I would be interested in working at the Mennonite Information Center. I know I need to look for employment. I had quit my former job four months before Ike's death so that I could be more available to help with some church projects. But without Ike's weekly paycheck, necessity demands I go job searching again.

The position at the Center sounds interesting and maybe this is the direction in which the Lord is leading me. He has been so wonderful to me these past weeks and I've been overwhelmed with all the cards, letters, phone calls, and money that I'm still receiving daily. Hundreds of people have written that they are praying for me. God is more real to me than He's ever been before and I have such peace in spite of the painful times when I miss Ike so badly.

January 23, 1990

Last night I dreamed that Ike returned. I told him he'd been gone a long time and I reached out to put my arms around him, but there was a strange distance between us and I couldn't get close to him. He looked at the picture of himself setting on the piano and said, "Nice picture." I relayed the dream to Dolores and she laughed, saying, "He could have said something more profound." Ike was always fun loving and enjoyed teasing and it was so much like something he would have said. The realization that he was never coming back hit me harder than ever before and I broke into tears. She held me until it was over.

Martin had to return to Costa Rica but Dolores and Derick are staying several more weeks. How I will miss them when they leave. The children have been such a support and comfort. Dawn and Donna took turns sleeping with me the first week so I wouldn't have to immediately encounter the empty side of the bed. It was thoughtful of them and helped tremendously to ease the transition to single life. I'm thankful for the four wonderful children the Lord has blessed me with.

Many people have told me in person and by letter how God has been speaking to them through Ike's death. I pray that the results will not just be a little rippling of their emotions which will soon be forgotten but rather a permanent change in their lives.

January 30, 1990

How I look forward each day to my faithful mailman's deliveries. He never disappoints me. I've received many cards and letters from people who have experienced losses of their own. One letter said,

> *I have found in life there is death. In January, 1989 four of my family were killed in a plane crash. With God's help we keep moving on.*

Another wrote,

> *I too, lost a family member in 1989 and his name was also Ike. But he wasn't my husband; he was my precious ten-year-old son who lost his battle with that dreaded disease, cancer. I pray life without your husband will be a blessing, maybe in a way you do not understand yet. God always has His reasons behind what He allows to happen.*

Yesterday a stranger called and said the Lord told him I was to marry him. Knowing he must have been an emotionally disturbed individual and having no success dissuading him,

I ended the conversation by hanging up the phone. I also received several letters from prisoners who wanted me to write and be their special friend. I felt so vulnerable as I realized my name, picture and address had been widely circulated through the news media and any unbalanced person, knowing my husband is gone can easily find me. I allowed fear and doubt of God's protection to overpower me. The Lord gave me this verse, "You will keep in perfect peace him whose mind is steadfast, because he trusts in You." Isaiah 26:31 "Lord, help me to keep my focus on You."

February 1, 1990

Last night I was home alone. I decided to watch TV, but that empty chair where Ike always sat kept shouting at me.

I'm thankful that Loren will be living here with me, at least for awhile. After one year at college, he began to feel unsure of which degree he should pursue and decided to drop his studies temporarily. He moved home and took a job locally. I see God's hand in that now.

February 8, 1990

My sister-in-law and I made a two-day visit last week to my brother Dick and his wife, Barbara, in northern Pennsylvania. I drove for the entire four and a half-hour trip because she isn't accustomed to a stick shift. When we arrived I was completely exhausted. It was difficult to participate in the conversation and I couldn't wait to get away by myself and rest. When I felt I could ask to be excused for a nap, I was so tired and miserable that I laid on the bed and cried uncontrollably. I suspect they would have liked to talk about Ike and what happened;

but if I'd had to discuss it then, I would have completely fallen apart. After resting awhile I got up for supper, but I had a headache and wished for nothing more than to go back to bed.

I know Ike's death has taken it's toll on me physically and emotionally and I need to learn what my limitations are.

February 15, 1990

People are still calling and taking me out to eat almost daily. Sometimes we go out twice a day, although I haven't any appetite and am losing weight.

Tonight I went to dinner with my friends, Lem and Alta, and then went shopping at the mall. On my return home my eyes were drawn upward to the beautiful starlit sky. As I stood there I wondered what Ike was doing just then in heaven and I wished I could see exactly what it was like.

Looking at his picture on the dresser I can't believe that I'm actually learning to live without him. It's hard to imagine that in time his memory will fade in my mind. There's something inside of me that rebels at that thought, but still I know he's no longer mine and I have to let him go.

———

The director of the Mennonite Information Center called asking me to start working there. I'll need to do some homework in preparing for the job and read several books to be better informed about Amish and Mennonite history. There's a life-sized reproduction of the Hebrew tabernacle there and one of my duties will be to give a 45-minute tour to visitors. I need to know the exact measurements of the building and each piece of furniture, materials used to construct it, what it's function was to the Israelite people, and the spiritual applications of its physical features. I need to be acquainted with the offerings and sacrifices made there and also be able to direct tourists to wherever it is they wish to go. Imagine me, who can get lost in a doctor's office, trying to explain to others how to find their way through the maze of winding country roads running all directions in the county!

But it's good to have something like this to occupy my mind. It helps to keep the dark thoughts away. The Lord keeps sending new things into my life and I feel as though I'm taking a crash course on faith.

February 22, 1990

I've been kept so busy that I haven't had much time to dwell on Ike's death, but it seems that the tears have been coming much more freely lately.

It's hard to sit through the singing at church without tears. The songs have such a deep experiential meaning to me now.

The Sunday School lesson last week was on forgiving those who have wronged us. God has mercifully spared me the struggle with hatred or revengeful feelings towards Ike's murderers. Maybe it's partly because over the years of ministry in an urban church, we were exposed to the harmful, dreadful home situations in which many young people exist.

I know, in spite of the pain it has brought me, that my circumstances are much better than the men who took Ike's life. I wonder what kind of homes they come from and what their mothers are like. My prayer is that if the time comes that I must face them, I'll be able to maintain these same sentiments. Strangely, I found it more difficult to forgive a fellow Christian who wronged me in a less significant way than to forgive these two persons who have wronged me so greatly. I suppose it has to do with our expectations of others. I know a very important factor in my ability to forgive now is that so many people are praying for me.

Ike's father gave me a copy of a letter he received from a man visiting Miami over the time of the shooting. He wrote,

> *As I was watching the newscast, the Miami news-people interviewed Isaac's daughter, Donna. I was overwhelmed with praise and humbled by the profundity of that woman's witness; a great sadness, but not bitterness. She had a calm assurance of God's presence. I was deeply touched. My thought was, if her father could see how his daughter is handling this tragedy before the world, he would be proud. Clearly, this daughter was raised by a godly father.*

I could tell this letter was comforting to my in-laws. Losing a second child in such a short time and in such traumatic ways has been difficult for them. I, too, am grateful that the children have accepted their Dad's death with such positive attitudes. It has been a terrible shock to them, but I haven't sensed any hostility or anger.

Several people have told me it's surprising that my life wasn't taken as well as Ike's, since I would be able to identify those who committed the homicide. I don't know why God spared my life but I know it was for a reason. I know there is something God wants of me here on this earth. I want to make my life useful—to encourage and help others.

February 27, 1990

I told God I wanted to be available to be used any way He chooses. Recently a man called asking if I would be willing to give my testimony about my experience in some churches this fall and I consented to do so. Fall seems far away; maybe I'll be able to handle it by then. I pray that when the time comes for those speaking engagements, I will be able not only to encourage people by sharing what God has done for me, but also challenge them to live closer to God and to be faithful in praying for others. I would like them to see how effective our prayers are for each other. I've felt the strength of those prayers in such a powerful way these past two months.

Mail continues to arrive daily. It comes from as wide a spectrum as Governor and Mrs. Casey to people serving prison terms. It still seems unbelievable that Ike's death has attracted so much attention. Who can understand God's ways?

I've begun working at the Information Center and have discovered my stress tolerance level is very low. It was an extremely difficult day and I found myself fighting back tears frequently. The two ladies I was working with couldn't have been more kind and helpful, but the tension of trying to learn and remember so many new things when I'm already so emotionally stretched is pushing me to my limits. After I've mastered the responsibilities of the job, I'm sure I'm going to enjoy it, but for now I'm glad I only need to work one day this week.

Donna came by this evening and took Loren and me out to dinner. Her thoughtfulness turned a depressing day into a good one.

March 1, 1990

"Peace I leave with you; my peace I give you. I do not give to you as the world gives. Do not let your heart be troubled and do not be afraid." John 14:27. These words have certainly taken on a new meaning. They are so gentle and compassionate and immersed in such intense love.

———————

I've missed Ike dreadfully these past few days. Irvin and Grace (my oldest sister) invited me for dinner. Afterwards everyone else was leaving for home with their husbands, but I was going home without mine. I cried the whole way. How glibly and thoughtlessly I'd sung songs about sorrow and pain. Now I'm learning the meaning of those words.

My friends have been loyal and thoughtful. But even the presence of dearest friends can't dissolve the loneliness that engulfs me. I never realized it was possible to feel so alone in a group of people, because of the absence of one individual; when that individual was the most important person in my life. In the end, this is a trip one must take alone, I suppose. Alone. But not without the presence of the only One who is truly able to penetrate loneliness.

March 7, 1990

I always thought the song, "My Jesus as Thou Wilt" was beautiful and would like it to be played at my funeral. I never anticipated that Dawn and Dolores would be playing it on their violins for Ike's funeral instead.

> My Jesus, as thou wilt. Oh, may thy will be mine.
> Into thy hands of love, I would my all resign.
> Through sorrow or through joy, conduct me as thine own.
> And help me still to say, my Lord, thy will be done.
>
> My Jesus, as thou wilt, though seen through many a tear,
> Let not my star of hope, grow dim or disappear.

Since thou on earth has wept and sorrowed oft alone,
If I must weep with thee, my Lord, thy will be done.

My Jesus, as thou wilt, all shall be well for me.
Each changing future scene, I gladly trust with thee.
Straight to my home above, I travel calmly on.
And sing in life or death, my Lord, thy will be done

> *Words by Benjamin Schmolk, 1716;*
> *translated by June Borthwick, 1854;*
> *music by Carl M. vonWeber, 1821.*

This is my prayer.

March 15, 1990

The birds are fun to watch. The cardinals were brilliant in their red coats as they ate at the feeder this morning. It reminded me of the time I knocked on the window to frighten the starlings and prevent them from devouring my bird food. How surprised they were, as was I, when my hand went right through the window pane. Ike, ever so patiently, advised, "Next time let the starlings have the bird food," as he replaced the broken windowpane.

How my life has changed since then. At times I feel as though I am experiencing reincarnation. I'm no longer Betsy Martin, ordinary housewife and mother. Now I'm this stranger, known as the woman whose husband was shot. Will I ever learn to live with this painful new identity?

March 22, 1990

Murder is such a cold cruel word. I've noticed people avoid using it. Some of them talk about my husband's "accident." No one feels comfortable saying he was murdered.

I've been reading about the children of Israel; about how strong their faith was after seeing God part the powerful waves of the Red Sea for them to cross. But then, it was only three days journey into the wilderness when they began to complain and doubt God because they didn't have water. I know I am too much inclined to emulate their behavior. God has been so close to me these past months. He's met all my emotional and physical needs in such a fantastic way. Yet there are times when I begin to worry and wonder how I am going to survive. It would be all too easy to doubt God even though He has brought me through all this. I pray God will grant me the faith I need.

March 29, 1990

I'm enjoying my job very much. It exposes me to many interesting people from varied cultural and geographical areas. Also it gives me a fresh appreciation for the Old Testament as I give the lectures about the tabernacle. One day a lady called from a western state saying she would like to marry an Amish man and requested we send her a list of names of eligible men and their addresses. My quick-thinking co-worker, who answered the phone, told the woman that she has been living in Amish country over sixty years, and has not been able to catch one for herself! I can tell this will be an interesting place to work.

My children continue to bless me with their love and concern. Loren asked if Sundays are difficult; and evenings he frequently inquires how my day has gone.

Donna stops by every few days and Dolores and Dawn call regularly to check on me. I've always been the parent concerned about their welfare. We seem to have reversed roles now but I don't mind.

Sunday was easier this week. It was the first time that I could sit through the service without tears, and that heavy lump of lead I've been carrying in the pit of my stomach, since Ike's death, has lightened a bit.

April 6, 1990

Today I removed my wedding ring from my finger. My hand looks bare like the feeling in my soul. It's hard to battle this persistent depression. I've often been told that holidays and special days such as birthdays and anniversaries are the worst, but I determined I wasn't going to let them get me down. It's not been easy with Easter, Ike's birthday, and our anniversary all coming in close succession.

I went out to his grave for the first time and it hurt so badly. This probably wasn't a good time to do that. It only gave the depression an opportunity to form a tighter grip. In spite of it all, God has been good and I've not been forgotten. I received five dinner invitations for Easter and three friends brought flowers.

Donna invited me to see a performance of the Easter story at her church. It was done expertly and the story was very meaningful. I've developed a new respect and appreciation for the pain Jesus endured for me. My pain is inconsequential in comparison.

April 13, 1990

Some of my family came and tore the old roof off the house and the following day twenty-five friends and relatives installed a new one. It was one of the tasks Ike planned to have done when we returned from Florida. Saturday our neighbor, Melvin Glick, and his friend replaced some leaking plumbing in the basement.

His wife and another neighbor appeared at the door with a large donation of money from the folks on our block. "Lord, give me a spirit of thankfulness and help me to focus on positive things."

April 19, 1990

Today would have been Ike's fiftieth birthday. When the children were younger they loved to serenade the birthday member of the family with the old familiar "Happy Birthday to You." However they created their own rendition by singing as off-key and torturous to the ear as possible. Somehow maturity didn't wean this one out and it remains a Martin family tradition. How embarrassed we were when Dolores brought Martin home to celebrate her birthday and meet her family for the first time. We thought on this one occasion for the sake of their oldest sister, they would certainly try a more melodious way to express their birthday wishes. But that was not to be. Instead they burst forth with the most obnoxious performance ever! However, Martin did return and eventually married her. Ike remarked, "It must be true love." I wonder if he is remembering that today. I suppose birthday celebrations don't exist in heaven since we never grow old there.

April 26, 1990

My father gave me a tape he made composed of songs, poems, and Bible verses telling of God's love and compassion for His children when they are suffering. I was deeply touched. My father was always a quiet, stern man and I was somewhat frightened of him in my childhood. Looking back, I can under-stand why he always seemed too preoccupied to pay attention to us children. He's had a difficult life. His first wife died when he was twenty-seven years old, leaving him with three small children. Several years later he married my mother who was a widow and mother of seven. The two of them became parents of five more, of which I am second to the youngest. World War II rationing compounded the difficulty of feeding and clothing such a brood. My mother died eight days after my tenth birthday, leaving him widowed with young children for the second time.

At age forty-seven, my father married again and had one more child. Somehow this disjointed family melded together and now they are such a support to me as I face my own hardships. My father has mellowed as he's grown older and it's easier to visit with him now. But it's still difficult to get past the reserve of my childhood years. I've never felt as close to him as I do since Ike died. He hugged me and cried when he and my stepmother came to the house. I know after all he's gone through, he understands. I can sense it in the tone of his voice as he reads those verses on the tape.

April 30, 1990

I received a sad letter today. It was from a woman whose daughter was murdered. She wrote,

> *Dear Mrs. Martin,*
> *I have started many letters to you, but have been unable to complete them. I know of your loss and my heart aches for you.*
> *You are most fortunate in finding comfort in your faith in God. As for me, I feel as though He has forsaken me. He did not even allow me to look upon my child's face one last time. My heart is broken and time is not healing it. The pain is actually worse as acceptance sets in. I have lost my first born and my daughter has lost her sister.*

*Even the love of family and friends has failed
to comfort us. If there is a merciful God may He not
grant forgiveness to the person who took my
daughter's life. Please pray for me, as I am unable to
pray for myself.*

How very, very difficult it must be to face tragedy without God.

May 7, 1990

Today would have been our thirtieth wedding anniversary.
I was only nineteen and Ike was barely twenty when we were
married. We were young, but we felt quite capable of taking on
that serious commitment and responsibility. We had our share of
disagreements and problems, but they were far outweighed by
the joy and satisfaction of our life together. How much I took for
granted! I never expected it to end so soon and so quickly.

May 15, 1990

A friend invited me to go with her to a banquet for singles.
I felt out of place for I still feel married. I don't belong at a single's
meeting. I don't want to belong. Evidently I haven't yet passed
the denial stage of grief.

May 23, 1990

I'm trying to be more consistent about my daily walks. Ike
and I always went together and it was painful to go alone at first.
Hiking down the back road through the countryside past our
development was something I'd always thoroughly enjoyed. The
Amish farms are neat and well-kept. The beauty of their simple
unadorned buildings is enhanced by the brilliantly-colored

flowers in their spacious gardens. I love going out when the sun is setting and one can see the silhouettes of the Amish men in the distance plowing the fields with their teams of horses.

Engaging in exercise every day tires me physically so I can go to sleep quickly at night. I haven't had any more bad dreams since the one soon after Ike's death. Several people told me they were going to pray that I'd never have another frightening dream or flashback of the murder. God heard and answered their prayers.

June 7, 1990

As I stepped outside the house, I realized flower planting time was upon me. The excitement and anticipation of watching small plants turn into lovely clumps of color that I normally experience this time of year is lacking. It's springtime outside. It's still winter in my spirit.

June 15, 1990

I found a copy of an old *Lancaster Mennonite Conference News* in which Ike's article "My Pilgrimage" was printed. It was written almost seven years ago, but it reveals who Ike was until the day his life on earth ended.

MY PILGRIMAGE
Isaac Martin
— **September 1, 1982** —

The setting for my pilgrimage began many years before I was born. Beginning with my birth in a godly home, where our lifestyle was based on Christian principles, my pilgrimage was being influenced with little choice on my part. The prayers at mealtime and the regular Sunday morning drives in the old Pontiac to the New Holland Mennonite Church helped impress me early with the fact that God is for real and cannot be ignored.

My knowledge of the Bible in my elementary and teenage years was less than the best. But Bible principles, as they were understood in my home, were to be obeyed and never compromised.

I remember the annual evangelistic services at church, the invitation hymn, and the increased heartbeat as the battle of conviction raged within. I remember my father asking if I thought the Lord was asking me to respond to the invitation, and my evasive reply to the question I didn't want to answer. My sister, Mary Alice, asked me the same question later, and I promised her I would respond at the next opportunity. That Saturday evening, at the age of thirteen, I gave my life to the Lord. I experienced a new peace as I went through a period of instruction and was baptized.

Much of the peace I was experiencing came from my new relationship with God, but some was the result of doing what was traditionally proper. To say that my life took on a new and drastic change would not be true. Rather, the change occurred in a gradual way over a period of many years as I grew in my relationship with God.

Involvement with the youth group of our church was an important part of my pilgrimage in my teen years. We sang for the old people at the Twin Linden Home in Churchtown; delivered a religious pamphlet, "The Way," to homes in New Holland; held monthly meetings and social activities such as parties and hay-rides.

After my childhood and adolescent years, the event which probably had the greatest impact on my life was courting and marrying Betsy. Her values and priorities were the same as mine and so it seemed like a wise decision to ask her to be a part of my life.

The stresses of establishing a new home, feeding unwilling babies Gerber's peas, changing and washing out dirty diapers while Betsy worked part-time, put a new dimension into my pilgrimage.

After attending a large church for the first thirty years of my life, the decision to move our membership to the small Vine Street Mission changed my life considerably. Besides meeting many new people, I was overwhelmed by all the needs and opportunities as we became involved in an urban church. Our responsibilities as youth advisors helped me relate to a much wider range of people than before.

We learned of the need for additional personnel at Laurel Street. Our decision to help fill that need was another move of faith on our part. The new beginning, in a small group deeply committed to the Lord and to each other, taught me a great deal about the effectiveness of a caring, united church.

At this point in my pilgrimage, I look forward with great confidence, knowing our Lord has not brought us this far to abandon us. God is faithful!

June 29, 1990

Pain—Lord, help me to stop fighting it. Help me to let it be there and allow You to minister to me through it. In spite of my resolution to not let it happen, holidays are depressing. It seems every time one makes an appearance, I go through several days of severe blues. The extreme heat and humidity add their force to my misery. I'm trying to stay on top of it and force myself into activities even though I don't feel like doing a thing.

I agreed to speak at three churches in September and I'm trying to prepare for that, but now it seems too emotionally draining and I think I'd better let it go for awhile.

July 4, 1990

Traveling in a bus has been a source of calamity in my life more than once. I remember a Fourth of July trip to New York City many years ago. Ike and I had taken thirty kids from the youth group on a one-day tour of the city in a rented bus.

The climax of the trip was to see the fantastic fireworks display over the water in Manhattan that night. It was close to midnight when our tribe, weary from a fun but exhausting day, went plodding back to the bus for our return to Lancaster. Imagine our astonishment when on arriving at the parking lot we discovered the bus was gone. The lot attendant had also disappeared and we stood in the center of the parking lot wondering what to do. Fortunately two of the youths with us had previously worked in a voluntary service program in New York and knew where the building housing the volunteers was located. So after praying for the Lord's protection, we led our weeping, frightened girls and outwardly courageous young men into a subway headed for the other side of town. Ike and one of the youth rode with the police to the station to file a report on the stolen bus. Our group arrived safely at the Voluntary Service Center, but it was approximately two hours later when Ike and Rob found their way to the house. Even though I was busy calling parents and getting everyone bedded down on the floor for the night, the hours they were gone seemed eternal to me. Knowing the dangers they might face on the street late at night, I prayed incessantly for their safe return. How relieved I was when I heard their voices at the door.

I prayed even more desperately for Ike's life in Miami, but God's response was different this time. Am I able to accept "no" as readily as "yes" from the Lord?

August 7, 1990

In August when the children were still living at home, we always spent a week at my sister, Lela, and brother-in-law Henry's dairy farm doing their chores while they went on vacation. Ike and I both grew up on farms and harbored pleasant, nostalgic memories of our childhood years which surfaced as we strolled out through the meadow to bring in the cows or when we fed the calves and cats in the barn. Even the bad farm odors attacking our nostrils as we cleaned up after milking never dampened our enthusiasm for that adventurous week on the farm. Located in a valley surrounded with green wooded hills, it had an aura of beauty and serenity which refreshed our souls after the often hectic schedules we kept at home. The children loved exploring the barn and tending the animals. It was an annual experience the whole family looked forward to with anticipation.

Through the years, school tuition, orthodontic braces, music lessons, etc. often kept our budget tight, yet we always found the resources and the time to take a family trip in addition to our week with the bovines. Sometimes we'd go camping in our big blue tent. Ike enjoyed life and he especially enjoyed spending time with his children. He was proud of them and tried whenever possible to attend Loren's baseball and basketball games and the girls' concerts and Bible quiz competitions.

I remember the time that Dawn played a violin solo for her high school spring concert. Before the event she went to the library in town to complete a homework assignment. Although her time was limited, she decided to shop for a blouse she felt was essential for her performance that night. After her purchase she dashed to the car, only to find that it would not start. Her father, already having barely enough time to dress for the evening, rushed to her rescue. We barely made it to the school auditorium before the concert began.

"She'll be so flustered she won't be able to play," Ike and I said to each other, but Dawn played the solo beautifully and compliments flowed freely.

Reflecting on parenting, Ike questioned, "How is it possible to be so frustrated with them one minute and so proud of them the next?"

August 16, 1990

I've been given many opportunities to tell people of God's love since Ike's death. At the Information Center sometimes we are short of guides for Amish tours of the county and on occasion I've been helping fill the void. I'm often put in a position to tell of my own personal relationship with Christ and I pray that God will use my testimony to bring the people I take on tour to faith in God as well.

August 23, 1990

It was beautiful again this evening as I went for my walk. The sun was going down with tints of blue and pink and the air was cool after a hot summer day. I loved the smell of hay and corn in the air. Queen Anne's lace and chicory grew by the side of the road and the spring peepers were chirping loudly. Life seemed enjoyable again. Mrs. Miller, my Amish neighbor, always saves vegetables or bakes bread and cake to give to me when I walk by her house. Anna, another neighbor, brings fresh corn from her garden. They are all kind and helpful and I think how I would miss them if I ever moved away.

September 6, 1990

Another letter came from a prisoner today. He wrote,

> *I pray that this letter finds you well and that I might reveal the power of God's love in my life. You see . . . your story in the Highway News is a story which has touched my heart deeply. I am in the Montgomery County Prison awaiting transfer to the State prison. The reason is because I attempted to harm a person in the course of a robbery. This person almost died of a serious wound to his heart in 1985. I found Jesus in April 1988 and in August 1989, I felt God move me to confess after four and a half years to this and to face the results. I fully trusted God that day and I trust Him even now. I received a sentence of five and a half to twelve years. But I do not fear this because I have Jesus Christ in my life. Jesus is faithful and just and shall guide me in the paths of God's will. I will also pray for you and my prayer is that those responsible for your husband's death may find and accept God's love and become responsible workers of God.*

I pray too, every day that the men will be led to someone who will share God's love with them. I know nothing is beyond God's power and no one is beyond His love and compassion.

September 13, 1990

Before my last tabernacle tour at work today, a lady came to the counter and engaged in a conversation with me. She saw my name tag and noting that we had the same name, she asked about my family. Upon learning I was Ike's widow, she called her friend from across the room who was from Miami. She said she walks by the spot where Ike was killed on her way to work every day. Each time she passes by she prays for me, but she never expected to meet me. It was such an encouragement.

September 20, 1990

The past few days have been more difficult again. Sunday morning I must give my first speaking assignment, but I wonder if I can bless anyone else with my story when I myself am weighted down in discouragement.

———————

Last weekend I went on a camp-out with my brothers and sisters and their spouses. When we are all together, the void left by Ike's death seems much more obvious.

I met an individual who introduced herself and said she recognized me from the news as the woman whose husband was killed. That happens frequently and sometimes I can handle it, but other times it's like acid on an open wound. This was one of those times and I went outside and began crying. The tears ran uncontrollably as I walked the grounds trying to avoid being noticed.

My sister, Ruth Ann came out and walked with me. She asked, "Are you sure you're ready to begin those talks next week?"

"No, I'm sure I'm not," I answered. She said she'd pray for me.

October 2, 1990

God is good. The depression and discouragement are gone and I feel as though a great load has been lifted off my shoulders. It's been replaced with peace and joy. I'd been worrying about my speaking assignment at Landis Valley Church, fearing I'd lose control of my emotions, embarrassing myself and everyone in the audience.

However, the evening before I was listening to a man on the radio telling his experiences after suffering an almost fatal heart attack. He became emotional and his voice broke numerous times.

God seemed to be showing me there was nothing wrong with showing emotion and I decided if it happened to me it was O.K. Many people said they would be praying that God would give me strength and calmness as I spoke and I could feel that they were. The tears came once or twice while I was speaking, but people in the congregation were crying too. It didn't appear to make them uncomfortable and after the service many of them told me that my words had helped them greatly. How useless it is to worry. Why do I have such difficulty learning that?

October 8, 1990

My friend, Anna Grace, and I went to an old fashioned hymn sing at the historical Alleghenyville church where I attended services as a small child. Lacking plumbing or electricity and with only a single board as a backrest on the benches, the tiny stone building was not designed for comfort.

It was packed with people and the walls reverberated with their voices as they sang those wonderful, precious old time songs of heaven. Again, my emotions would not be controlled and no matter how hard I tried to restrain the tears, they refused to be checked.

After a period of singing, the congregation was given a brief intermission to rest our voices. A man walked by where I was sitting and asked if the purse by my side belonged to me. I nodded and he reached down and stuffed a wad of bills into it. When I got home I counted $500.00.

Our family plans to spend Christmas in Costa Rica with Dolores and her family and the money will cover the cost of my plane ticket. What surprising and unexpected ways God uses to meet my needs.

October 16, 1990

My speaking assignment this week was at a church requiring a three-hour drive. Wanting to be sure we were on time, my sister, Lillian, and I left the house rather early. We decided to stop for breakfast on the way, so after driving several hours we had a good hearty meal at a cozy little restaurant.

Back on the road, we drove for another fifty minutes. Realizing that we were going to arrive at our destination much too early, we found another restaurant and enjoyed another breakfast. We drove into the church parking lot at just the right time and with very full stomachs.

November 2, 1990

In our early dating years, Ike and I formed a close friendship with three other young couples. We retained that relation-

ship into our adulthood and made it a priority to get together
for a weekend at the mountains every year. Our busy schedules
often prevented us from seeing each other outside of this annual
event, so it was a good time to catch up on what was going on in
our lives and to celebrate old times. I was dreading the reunion
this year because I am now only half a couple and it is painful to
have to face it so forcefully, as at times like this.

But it turned out to be an enjoyable weekend. We had a
rewarding time together, sharing things of real importance to us.
It's interesting how a death in our midst weeds out so much of
the clutter in our hearts and minds.

November 7, 1990

I received a request to appear on the program "Live on
WGAL" TV. The subject of discussion was dealing with grief
over the holidays. Feeling that this could have some positive
value, I agreed to participate. So, accompanied by Donna, I wound
my way to the TV station on the hill. The members of the panel
besides myself were the talk show host, a psychiatrist, and a
mortician. We were briefed on the format of the show and wired
to the platform with microphones. On the air the host asked me
if I had gone for counseling after Ike's murder. I replied that I
hadn't, but that I relied on my faith in God and was blessed with
a very supportive family, friends, and church.

My statement was followed by a commercial break, so the
point wasn't pursued. I hoped that my words wouldn't cause anyone who may have been watching to hesitate going for counseling if they are in need of it, or gave the impression that if they
do they are not trusting God. I know that I've had an unusual
amount of prayer support and help from others which not everyone receives. The day may come when I will feel the need of

counseling or medication and I believe God uses these as
well for helping His children find their way back to healing and
wholeness.

November 14, 1990

I have shared my experiences about Ike's death six times
so far and am getting calls for more speaking engagements.

I was reading in my devotions from II Samuel where God
told David that he would become king and how God would use
him. David was surprised and in amazement responded by saying, "Is this the usual way You deal with man?"

After all the events of the past eleven months those words
verbalize what I sometimes feel. The unusual paths into which
the Lord has been leading me seem unbelievable. I've had so
many blessings through it all, but at times the pain of losing Ike
is still so acute I find myself wishing I could go back and have
things the way they used to be. I know that will never happen
and just wishfully looking back makes the pain more severe.
I need to look forward, keeping my relationship with God as
intact as possible so that He can truly fulfill His purpose in me.

November 22, 1990

During their elementary and high school years, our three
daughters played their violins and also sang together accompanied by Ike on his guitar. Periodically we presented music and
puppet programs in churches in the area.

A friend sent a tape to me which her husband had recorded
at a Thanksgiving service at her church many years ago, in which
our family participated. It was thoughtful of Helen to send the
recording now that Ike is gone.

The children enjoyed listening to it as much as I did and it brought back many memories; scenes of past music lessons and practices for programs. I always believed that if our audiences had heard the arguments about which pieces should or should not be included in the program or who was singing or playing out of tune, no one would have allowed us through their church doors. Once, in the confusion which resulted from gathering musical instruments, mikes, and puppet equipment for a program, we arrived at a church to discover that no one had thought to bring the music. We pulled our impromptu performance together as quickly as we could with pieces we felt we could manage by memory.

As the children and I listened to ourselves singing on that old Thanksgiving tape, we laughed at the barely discernible mumble in the background. That was the nonmusical member of the group—Loren. Although he proved to be a rather accomplished puppeteer in his younger years, his talent in music was either nonexistent or undeveloped. Initially we believed that with enough encouragement (we didn't like to think of it as coercion) he could be taught to play guitar like his father. Although Ike successfully taught other people's children to play proficiently, he finally conceded to failure in passing the skill to his own son. After a short stint with piano lessons, we accepted Loren's right to "be his own person" and let him alone to pursue his own interests of baseball and basketball.

Now Dawn has Ike's guitar. He won't be needing it anymore. Does he have a new golden one to play in heaven or does everyone play harps? I wonder.

November 28, 1990

In my devotions I read, "For I know the plans I have for you, declares the Lord; plans to prosper you and not to harm you, plans to give you hope and a future." Jeremiah 29:11. My heart was filled with peace as I read over it and let the words soak into my soul.

I continue to vacillate between periods of heavy sadness and peace and joy. May the Lord help me not to become tired of waiting for emotional healing because I know in the end this is all for my own good.

December 11, 1990

It's exactly one year since Ike was killed. The day made its debut with the most glorious sunrise. I can't recall ever having seen a more beautiful one. The whole sky was vibrant with color. Not wanting to miss a moment of it, I decided to take an early morning walk. I was impressed with the greatness of God and the love He must have for me to give such a gift of beauty.

My church had a memorial service for Ike on Sunday and asked me to speak. Five of his brothers and sisters came. Betty and Mary Alice live in other states and couldn't be there. It was a very emotional time for all of us, but it was good to sense the love and support from everyone in my church family.

A reporter from the *Lancaster New Era* also came, but I didn't know she was there. The following day a large headline story with our picture was on the front page. When I first saw it I resented what I felt was an intrusion on my privacy, but after I read the article I felt differently about it. The quotes were accurate and emphasized the spiritual aspect of my story — what I had said about God's faithfulness. I couldn't help but praise God for the way He takes over in spite of my selfish perspective of things. My understanding of His greatness and His love has become much clearer this past year.

Derick and Lisa—Dolores and Martin's children.

January 4, 1991

Loren, Donna and I spent the Christmas holidays in Costa Rica with Dolores and Martin. We met little Lisa, born on September 4. What a little doll she is with her head of silky black hair. Big brother Derick is now just one month shy of a mature three-year-old. Isn't it amazing that when a smaller addition makes an appearance into the family, older babies grow into little boy and girl status instantaneously?

How good it was to see them all again. A year is a long time to be separated from those you love. But we enjoyed each other all the more because our time together was limited. We all missed Dawn, but her graduate studies and impending wedding next August made it impossible for her to join us this time.

I was sitting in Dolores' kitchen when I heard a loud noise similar to a locomotive roaring through the house. The walls began to sway, the floor moved and articles fell off the shelves. Water splashed out of the fish aquarium as the realization hit me that I was experiencing a major earthquake. I dashed outdoors where a giant land-wave resembling the ocean rolled across the lawn in sync with my stomach. It was all over in seconds and my heart reverted to a more normal beat. Throughout the day and into the night aftershocks kept my "earthquake rookie" family and me on edge. Dolores reassured us that aftershocks were good signs, for when they don't appear there is a high probability of another larger quake. We learned that fortunately the epi-center of this seven-point quake was in a sparsely populated mountain area so that only one fatality occurred. We drove to San Jose to view the damage there. It was mostly broken glass from store windows, cracked streets and sidewalks, but there was structural damage to some buildings. The Costa Ricans are wise to build their homes solidly to withstand quakes and minimize damages.

Costa Rica is a beautiful country. The weather is comfortable year round, the mountains are eternally green, and the beaches are clean and expansive. It's soothing to the spirit to sit on the sand watching the waves with scarcely a soul to be seen on shore. In the distance, fishermen pulled their nets into their boats.

Flowers bloom profusely everywhere, mirroring the small brightly-colored homes surrounded with decorative iron fences. The people are warm and friendly even though my Spanish is limited to a few words and phrases. Their slower, more casual pace of life is refreshing and I could feel myself unwinding after being there for just a couple days—that is, in the absence of earthquakes.

We had a typical Costa Rican Christmas where the tradition is to have Christmas dinner and open gifts at midnight. We ate tamales (ground meat seasoned with chili, rolled in cornmeal dough, wrapped in banana leaves and steamed), rice and refried beans. There were delicious cold drinks made from fresh tropical fruit juices. It's fun to experience other cultures but I still prefer turkey, stuffing, and mince pie.

We had a wonderful time there with all the family. Too soon it was time to return to the states—back to work and schedules.

January 11, 1991

I was approached by another shopper in the grocery store. She said she read the article in the *New Era* and wondered about the things I'd been quoted as saying. It was difficult for her to understand how anyone could actually forgive in circumstances such as mine. I told her God forgave me and He enabled me to forgive others, even for such a horrific wrong as these men had committed. I'm thankful that God has given the blessing of forgiveness. Grudges and revengeful feelings are such heavy burdens to carry.

January 18, 1991

I've never experienced depression before; bad moods, yes, but not this heaviness that conquers my most adamant resolve to keep it at bay. I suppose I still don't really know what depression is. I've never had to endure the deep, debilitating mental anguish some people suffer for months on end. The sun does break through the clouds frequently no matter how dark they seem at times.

I know it isn't wise to spend too many hours alone. I need time for introspection, but I can become ingrown if it's overdone. My goal is to become involved in the lives of others who need someone. It's important for me to make plans—things I need to get up and do whether I feel like it or not.

I've been bombarded with temptation this week. It makes me wonder what it was like for Jesus when He spent forty days in the wilderness being tempted.

It started on Sunday. I'm teaching the fifth-graders in Sunday School and Victor was being difficult all morning. When he wasn't talking loudly, he'd disrupt the class by muttering unintelligibly under his breath in what seemed to be a deliberate attempt to block out my words. He bragged about hiding a stolen gun under his jacket at school, which the teacher found but claimed he still had his knife. I don't know if what he said was true or only an attempt to impress the other students, but it made me ill that this is the kind of behavior he admires and wants to emulate. It reminded me of the young men in Miami who bragged about killing Ike to get respect from their peers. What a sad state of affairs when one must gain his self esteem through inflicting pain on others. However I know that Victor is only expressing his own pain as he's been abused and unloved all his life. It's a challenge to penetrate the hard shell in which he's wrapped himself to avoid revealing his vulnerability. I pray that I may be instrumental in showing him genuine love and acceptance and that he will be able to absorb the fact that he is loved by God. However, this week I felt frustrated and impatient with him.

I have a lot of speaking engagements scheduled over the next months and when I'm in this kind of mood I feel as though I can't go through another one. I feel restless and wish for some normalcy in my life — some security, other than God's. Just like Peter, who was walking on the water towards Jesus, began to sink as he looked around at the storm and waves, I too, begin to sink; except for me, the storms are raging in my mind. Jesus took Peter's hand and said, "Why did you doubt?" I've felt Him do the same for me so many times and I know He will do it again. I can't gain victory over this dreadful attitude by myself, but my Lord will bring me through it if I trust Him. He's always kind and patient with me.

I received a card in the mail from a young adult group of a Lancaster County church. Each of them wrote little notes in response to the newspaper article in the *Lancaster New Era*. They said it had been a challenge and encouragement to them and that they are praying for me. I cried when I read it, for I've felt like such a failure these past few days. I haven't been a good example of God's love. Yet the Lord prompted those young people to write those notes at a time they were least deserved but needed most.

January 25, 1991

I had my first date since Ike died. It seemed all wrong. How very strange to think about dating again after being married twenty-nine years. Both dating and society are so different now. I don't even know if I should sit in the car and wait for the gentleman to come around and open the door for me or if I should just hop out by myself. Is there one set of rules for dating etiquette for my generation and another for younger people?

I don't feel ready to start a new relationship, but I hate to turn a man down. I hate having to inflict another wound on someone who is already suffering from the loss of his wife. It feels as though I've just added insult to injury.

The children agreed that I should wait—maybe five years. Loren advised me to stay single. He doesn't want it to be necessary for him to engage in the mental gymnastics I find myself involved in when explaining where each of my mixed-up batch of siblings fits into the family picture.

February 2, 1991

I traveled with three friends to visit Ike's sister Betty in Ohio for what we expected to be a weekend trip. We arrived Friday evening and the following afternoon took a long hike. Later we stopped for dinner where I had a huge platter of catfish for which that particular restaurant is famous. After eating I began to feel sick and it became obvious that my stomach wasn't enjoying the catfish to the degree that my taste buds had. Betty's soft, comfortable bed was a welcome sight, but sleep refused to come. I lay awake feeling miserable most of the night. I was scheduled to speak at the church in Ohio on Sunday morning, but instead found myself in the hospital having surgery for appendicitis. Some of the tissue surrounding my appendix was infected and gangrenous so I was hospitalized the entire week. The nurses were very kind and attentive, perhaps because I didn't know anyone in the area and the hospital was too far away for Betty to visit often.

Dawn is attending graduate school in Miami, Ohio, and took an afternoon off to visit me. How wonderful to see a familiar face. Many people from home called and my pastor Randy phoned every day.

After leaving the hospital, I spent another week at Betty's apartment before I was allowed to travel home. She worked every day and I filled in the time doing light housework for her, reading and taking walks. Some people from her church stopped in to see me occasionally. At the end of the second week my brother and sister-in-law, Sam and Janet, came from Pennsylvania to take me home. They made a bed for me in the back seat of their car and I had a very comfortable ride.

The friends with whom I'd taken the trip to Ohio had to return to their jobs immediately after my surgery. One of them, Anna, told me how badly she felt leaving me there. She has been a good friend, helping me become acclimated to single life, inviting me out with her friends and introducing me to new ones. Ike and Anna were cousins and she was the channel through which we met. We seriously considered her suggestion that we'd make a good couple and out of respect for her matchmaking skills, willingly obliged. Anna and I were two of a group of young girls who spent weekends having good times together. She was always the ingenious one who had a solution for any problem we might encounter.

On one occasion we were taking a weekend trip when the car's muffler tore loose, dragging loudly on the road beneath us. Anna opened her suitcase, pulled out the belt to her robe, crawled under the car and tied up the bothersome muffler. It worked perfectly—no more loud noises.

Then there was the time a certain gentleman was making a nuisance of himself by following us girls to our activities, hoping to pique our interest in him. Anna donned her father's big black hat and became a surreptitious boyfriend to another friend who sat beside her as they drove down the street. The rest of us crouched down on the floor of the car out of sight. The persistent suitor, we hoped, would see the affectionate couple and assume he had lost to the competition.

I often drove my stepmother's small Plymouth coupe and we were extremely resourceful in finding ways to accommodate all who needed a ride to whatever function we happened to be attending. Seat belts weren't on the scene back then, and on one of our overloaded excursions as we rounded a corner, the car door burst open. Anna, who was on the far right passenger seat, went with it. One friend grasped her legs and another one her arms, while the rest of her body remained on the exterior of the vehicle. I stopped the car as quickly as possible. We pulled Anna's whole self back inside and were on our way again.

After Ike and I were married, Anna and I spent less time together. But now she is always there, doing thoughtful things, helping make my life easier. Gladys Tabor in her book, *Stillmeadow Calendar* compares life to a garden, "times of ripening, times of harvest, times of ice and snow." Anna has been a loyal friend through all those times in my life. Everyone should have a friend like her.

February 10, 1991

I was asked to speak at a church located along a dark country road. I had been given accurate, easily understandable directions, but the small sign I was looking for eluded me in the darkness. I drove several miles before I felt certain I had missed it, so I turned around and retraced the route. Failing to locate my landmark after three attempts, I decided I needed help, so I looked for a likely place to obtain new directions. Time was progressing more rapidly than I; and I realized the service was about to begin. I had to drive several more miles before I could find a house with any sign of life. Approaching a state of panic, I restrained an urge to hug the lady who answered the door and informed me that she knew just the place I was looking for.

A half-hour late, breathless and with heart racing, I found the church. The congregation was singing and the man waiting for me at the door ignored my apologies, calmly saying, "Oh, we knew you'd be coming and we decided to sing until you arrived." Without a minute to pull myself together, I was introduced and promptly started my speech. What would I do without the Lord to settle me down at times like this?

Since Ike died, I sometimes feel bombarded with people who have problems of their own, or know someone they think would be helped if I could talk to them. I want to help them if I can, but I hope in my talks I'm not giving the impression that I have the answers to life's difficulties and have it all together. Nothing could be further from the truth. Many people tell me that I am an inspiration to them and sometimes it frightens me because I know all of my faults and weaknesses. I'm afraid they're setting me on a pedestal because of what I've been through and, if they do, I'll certainly disappoint them. I try to make them understand that it is only because of God's mercy and the prayers of many people that I have made it through these past months intact. I want to rely on God to live through me so that I can relax, not feeling that I must prove anything to anyone.

February 16, 1991

Lately I've been thinking more about the verse "And anyone who does not take his cross and follow Me is not worthy of Me." Matthew 10:38. I think my cross has been loneliness. I've missed Ike so badly and loneliness is intense sometimes even though I am with friends or family. Last night I awoke and turned on the radio by my bed. One song followed another with messages of God's love and faithfulness. They sang a song which has comforted me greatly through this ordeal; "Be Still My Soul."

Be still, my soul, the Lord is on thy side;
Bear patiently the cross of grief or pain;
Leave to thy God to order and provide;
In every change He faithful will remain.
Be still my soul, thy best, thy heavenly friend
Through thorny ways leads to a joyful end.

Be still my soul, thy God doth undertake
To guide the future as he has the past;
Thy hope, thy confidence let nothing shake;
All now mysterious shall be bright at last.
Be still my soul, the waves and winds still know
His voice who ruled them while He dwelt below.

Be still my soul, the hour is hastening on
When we shall be forever with the Lord.
When disappointment, grief, and fear are gone
Sorrow forgot, life's purest joys restored.
Be still, my soul, when change and tears are past,
All safe and blessed we shall meet at last.

- Katharina von Schlegel

I wept as I listened to the words. Finally I was able to go back to sleep. I must stop fighting loneliness and depression and be willing to carry it, just as Christ carried a much heavier cross for me.

February 27, 1991

In addition to my days at the center, I've begun part-time employment at the Mennonite Home. I worked there in therapeutic recreation before Ike died and it feels good to be back. My job is to plan activities for around 200 residents in personal care. Many of them I already know, but I've also met others who have arrived at the home more recently. I enjoy working with older people; they have a good perspective on life after years of varied experiences and their quaint sense of humor is delightfully entertaining.

I bought a smaller house and put our present one up for sale. Loren and I don't need this much room and the lawn work is becoming burdensome. I wanted a small Cape Cod, one with flower boxes at the windows and a lawn just large enough to grow some flowers, but without bushes to trim or a great deal of grass to mow. The house I found is perfect. The verse "And my God will meet all your needs according to His glorious riches in Christ Jesus," Philippians 4:19, has certainly proven true in my life. He goes far beyond my needs much of the time.

March 6, 1991

God has given me a ministry, I've been told, of strengthening others' faith by giving my testimony through speaking engagements. However, many times before I speak I feel overwhelmed with anxiety and temptations. Depression is striking full force again.

Occasionally, I've been having spells of lightheadedness and I'm afraid I'm passing my threshold of stress endurance. Awaking this morning at 2:00 a.m., I lay there while anxious unrelenting thoughts raced wildly through my mind. I've been allowing them that freedom too much of late and I find they are interfering with my ability to enjoy meaningful devotions. My over-stretched nerves will snap if they aren't relieved of this escalating tension that's been assuming control over me. I feel very close to the edge sometimes.

Last night, instead of lying there allowing my thoughts to wander unrestrained down their usual worrisome course, I got up and read my Bible and listened to a "Messiah" tape for an hour and a half. I could feel Satan fighting for control of my mind and again I realized how weak and helpless I am without God. If I am going to retain my sanity under all these pressures, I must keep our relationship as my first priority.

God felt close again as I absorbed the words in the scripture text and in the music. When my need is greatest, I feel Him the nearest. The only thing I need to fear is myself and my own proud tendency towards self-sufficiency. "Thank you, Lord, for helping me through one more battle." Satan can torment God's children, but he can't conquer them. I like to picture myself being held tightly in God's arms. There I feel safe.

March 13, 1991

Recently I bought a book on prayer by Charles Finney. I was impressed with the depth and effectiveness of his prayer life. He said we shouldn't allow our minds to dwell on our weaknesses, but on God's righteousness and His ability to give us His righteousness and sanctification.

I spoke to someone who lost his child through suicide. He wanted to know how I was able to bear Ike's death. I want to be sensitive to people's pain, but I want to maintain a balance — not to minimize the horror, awfulness, and pain of these things we go through, but not allow it to become too big either. I need to keep hold of the fact that God is greater than all this. I pray that God will help me empathize with the hurts of others but also help me communicate hope and victory in my conversations with them.

March 24, 1991

A letter came in the mail from a young Russian girl I'd taken on a Lancaster County tour last fall. She'd never been to church and knew very little about Christianity. She was with a group of students and time didn't allow for an extended conversation with her during the tour. After she'd pelted me with questions, I promised if she'd write, I would attempt by letter to help her learn more about our beliefs. We corresponded several times and I tried to explain to her God's plan of salvation in as simple terms as possible. One of her letters stated that she'd begun reading the Bible and today I received the joyful news. She announced, "I must tell you, I've accepted Christ and have been baptized." I have been praying for this since I met her.

I was reminded of the time at Ike's funeral when an unknown older woman, alone and quite ordinary looking with straight hair and rather plain face, came through the line to greet our family. She said to me, "I have a word from the Lord for you. Because of this experience people from far away places will come to know the Lord." It's true that if Ike hadn't died, I wouldn't be giving tours at the Information Center. Through this job, I have been able to tell people from many countries, including Olga from Russia, about my faith in God. I thought of the man from Costa Rica, who drove the bus which we had transported, bringing folks to church. Although not a Christian himself, he stayed for services until time to return the church members to their homes. Through his attendance he came to know the Lord and later brought the rest of his family to church as well. I've heard angels come in many disguises. Is it possible that an angel spoke this word to me?

April 4, 1991

I was shopping and saw some beautiful lilies for sale. Ike always bought a potted flower for me at Easter and I felt an urge to put one on his grave. As I placed it there in front of the pink marble tombstone I relived the tragic events that brought me to this place. How painful it was to think back over our life together and to know it's all part of the past now. It seemed incomprehensible that he'd been murdered and that my life has taken such a strange turn. I wondered why God chose to thrust me into this situation; it certainly isn't the plan I would have chosen. But whatever the reason, I will go on trusting Him. Sometimes life on this earth seems so sad and I can't wait to go to heaven and at other times it's rather intriguing to see what God will bring into my life next.

April 12, 1991

I'm reading *The Lover and The Beloved* by John Michael Talbot. He says we need some of Mary and Martha, both the active and the contemplative. It's easy for me to judge the success of my day by what I've been able to accomplish, rather than having kept my thoughts on Christ throughout the day.

Often I wish I could pray more effectively and without distraction. At first, after Ike died, I was able to concentrate on God easily because my emotional needs were so great, but now that my life is becoming more routine the distractions are increasing.

Talbot suggests that when distractions annoy us during prayer, we should pretend that we don't even notice their presence. He says if we submit our temptations to Christ they will often disappear. Instead of giving attention to them, we should relax and passively ignore them and often they will go away.

April 19, 1991

Last week after filling my gas tank, I drove away without paying. Twenty minutes after I arrived home, a policeman appeared at the door, asking if I'd bought gas lately. He smiled as my facial expression revealed that the truth was dawning on my cloudy brain; I'd forgotten to pay.

Then, the other day after doing some shopping, I crossed the parking lot, unlocked the car door and was climbing inside when a lady came dashing my way screeching, "That's my car!" Sure enough, three vehicles up the line an identical car was parked—same color, same model, same year, and with locks that opened with the same key. Only the license plate numbers were different, and with a very red face I walked toward it.

Today at work all culminated when, while calling the words at a spelling bee for the residents, my eyes dropped to my feet. In amazement I saw two differently colored shoes encasing them. "I was in a hurry when I dressed for work this morning," I rationalized to myself.

Later, one of my co-workers, rather discouraged and down-hearted, told me about several mistakes she'd made that day and her concern about them. I stepped back and directed her vision downward to my feet. She roared with laughter as she looked at my mismatched attire. It's nice to know we won't be lonely on the road to senility.

April 25, 1991

After I spoke at a church on Sunday morning, a young man approached me and said he had recently been released from prison for almost killing a man while under the influence of drugs. "Now I'm trying to get my life back together," he told me. But there was something in his demeanor and the way he spoke that gave the impression he didn't really regret his past life. I felt very uncomfortable while speaking with him and I wondered how I will react if someday I have to face the men who murdered Ike. I'm thankful that I don't have to deal with that now.

May 7, 1991

This is our second wedding anniversary since Ike is gone. I took a walk down by the creek this afternoon. The wild flowers were blooming, the birds were calling to each other, and the ducks were quacking softly as they paddled up and down the stream. I found a bed of my favorite flowers—violets. It was a beautiful gift from the Lord and I felt thankful for this lovely private place where I could find healing for my burdened heart. How I wished Ike would be there enjoying it with me. The heaviness didn't go away, but I did enjoy the beauty of that little bit of forest practically in my back yard.

Sometimes it is hard to enjoy even beautiful things and I wonder if I will ever be happy again. I find myself pleading, "Lord, won't it soon be enough?" But somehow it doesn't matter. God is with me and as long as I bring Him honor with my life, it doesn't matter if it seems sad and lonely much of the time. I know God won't require me to go on like this for always. Better times will come.

May 14, 1991

I had a talk scheduled, but the previous day I got a severe case of laryngitis. Feeling certain I wouldn't be able to speak for forty minutes I called to cancel. But the lady in charge said I should wait and see how I was by morning. They would pray that my voice would clear. It did and I was able to speak without a problem—the result of a faithful believing group of women.

May 21, 1991

I've been packing to move, but I am filled with mixed emotions. It will be difficult to leave this home that has been ours for twenty-four years. Many memories have germinated in and around this house.

Our three daughters were small; the youngest one only six months old when we moved in. The two oldest, aged three and four, although curious about the children next door, were too timid to make the first gesture of friendship. Equally bashful, the neighbor's little ones sat cross-legged at the edge of their property as Dolores and Donna settled down facing them at a three-foot distance. After examining and evaluating each other thoroughly for about five minutes, they jumped up and began to play together. The girls apparently were properly initiated into the neighborhood.

I remember the time when Donna, about four years old, came to the conclusion that she wasn't being treated well in this family and decided to seek her fortune in a new home. She made a peanut butter sandwich and, putting it into a paper bag, set out to see what better things the world had to offer. I watched unobserved as she crossed the neighbor's lawn. After walking several yards farther she sat down to eat her sandwich. Her last morsel of food gone, she continued her journey up a slight grade to the next neighbor's house where she stopped to play. About thirty minutes later she retraced her steps homeward. She crept softly in the door and eyeing us sheepishly, she picked up her dolls and began to play. We welcomed her back into the fold. Home wasn't such a bad place after all.

This house was new when we moved into it and being a tight structure, we had few problems with rodents making unwelcome entries. However, one night after we climbed into bed, a mouse suddenly made an appearance. Harboring a strong dislike for the nasty little creatures, I stood up on the bed as Ike picked up a shoe and chased the mouse about the room. Back and forth, this way and that, it went with Ike in hot pursuit. Finally when both man and beast were at the point of exhaustion, the invader was cornered in a closet, and came to a violent end by being struck with a size eleven shoe.

There are other stories, some happy and amusing, some involving anxious worrisome times, but all of them weaving the threads of our family's lives together in this house. Here we shared, loved, fought, and grew. Even though we are moving on and leaving the house behind, the love that binds us together will still be intact.

June 14, 1991

Here we are, Loren and I, settled into our new, little brown Cape Cod duplex with red shutters, a daylight basement that we plan to turn into bedrooms for the children when they visit, and a relatively small lawn. There's a steep bank in the back yard which will be perfect for sledding when the grandchildren visit this winter.

With the assistance of three of Loren's friends and several of my brothers and sisters, the move went smoothly. I love this tiny place. It will be fun adding some things here and there to make it home.

Loren is going to build some window boxes for my red, lavender, and white petunias and I think I'll plant some daisies and lilies around the mailbox. After all, the street on which we live is called Daisy Lane and we should do something to authenticate its name.

June 23, 1991

I met a man living at the Mennonite Home with whom I've become friends. He's very good in music and art, often playing piano or accordion at the weekly music programs I plan for the residents. In spite of his many talents, he is quiet, modest, and unselfish. He is a man of deep convictions, who feels no need to compete to get ahead of anyone else. He challenges me to grow spiritually and I think that is why I like him so much. I expect that we will never be more than friends because our lifestyles are so different, but I'm thankful that we have times to be together and talk.

July 12, 1991

Tonight, while stepping out of the car at the church where I was speaking, I lost my grip on my notes. They dropped to the ground beside me, and being a breezy evening, the wind quickly picked them up. In amazement I watched as they went sailing away in every direction over the parking lot and through the cemetery. When I rose to speak I announced to the congregation that my notes were blowing about throughout the churchyard. If they wished to know what I'd forgotten to include in my story they had my permission to gather and read them. "Lord, You certainly have interesting ways of teaching me to depend on You."

August 15, 1991

The house was lively and full of fun these past weeks with the children home and visitors stopping by. Dolores, Martin, and the children were here for Dawn and Brian's wedding and spent a week with us.

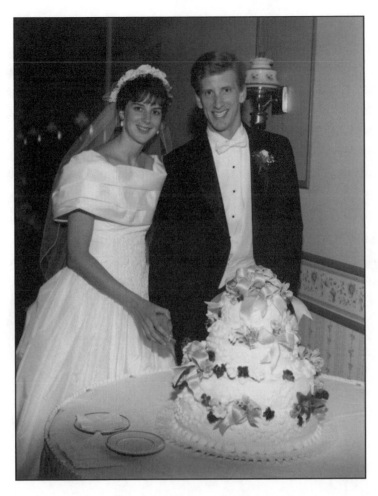

Dawn and Brian's wedding.

The wedding is over. It was beautiful. Dawn's degree in music served her well in planning this important day. The string and vocal quartets, cello solo, and Dolores and Martin's duet all combined to make it a truly memorable occasion.

Nothing gives me more joy and satisfaction than seeing my children first commit their lives to Christ and then find mates who share that commitment. Both Dolores and Dawn have chosen fine men who love the Lord and I now have two wonderful sons-in-law.

I wondered if Ike knew about our celebration. I wished that he had been there. Loren looked so tall and handsome as he led Dawn down the aisle to the altar, but I struggled to keep back the tears because it should have been her dad's arm she was holding. It was a day of intense emotions for me; sadness that Ike was absent, but joy that Dawn has found a strong man who loves her.

Dolores, Martin, and the children have returned to Costa Rica. Loren also has left for school in Arkansas. I was at work when he made his departure, but found this note on the kitchen sink when I came home.

> *Goodbye Mom,*
> *I made sure not to leave the house too clean*
> *so you won't miss me too much. Take care.*
> *I love you,*
>
> *Loren*

I miss them all, but I think I'll soon adjust to living by myself. Donna's apartment is only about five miles away and she stops by frequently, for which I am grateful.

August 23, 1991

I'm learning to take one day at a time, but I have a great deal of growing to do. Yesterday I read again in Psalm 138:8, "The Lord will fulfill His purpose for me. Your love, Oh Lord, endures forever; do not abandon the work of Your hands."

It's easy to allow other things to come before the Lord. How wonderful it would be to be free of this self, struggling for first priority in my affections.

September 10, 1991

I've been dating again, but I'm really not sure how I feel about remarrying. When I think of all it would entail, trying to combine two families and two households, I'm not sure I want to tackle all that. Marriage at this stage of my life is quite different and more complicated than the first time. I would not be marrying an individual only, but an entire family. I don't want to make a mistake in something that will affect my life and my children's in such a profound way.

September 21, 1991

Since Ike's gone, I have been taking classes part-time at Millersville University. One of my courses is Criminal Justice and the class took a tour of the Lancaster County Prison. It's sad to see how these men are imprisoned not only physically but spiritually. They are destroying their own lives and the lives of others. The gentleman who sits next to me asked what I thought of the tour. I said I found it depressing and in response to his question, "Why?", I told him about Ike. Remembering reading about it in the newspaper, he exclaimed, "I can't imagine going through something like that." I told him how God helped me and he seemed very receptive to my words.

It amazes me how people's attitudes seem to change when we drop superfluous subjects for serious ones such as death. I believe that people are concerned about where they are going and that they are conscious that there is more to life than is seen on the surface.

I've been feeling down lately—weak spiritually, as well as emotionally. It seems at these times is when God puts the opportunities there to tell about His grace and mercy. I'm again thankful that it's not through what we are or what strength we have, but through His strength and His wisdom that we are used.

October 8, 1991

I love October in Lancaster County when the leaves blaze into full and varied colors. Every fall I take at least one drive through the hills to enjoy them. The air is crisp and cool, causing me to feel invigorated and ambitious. I get an urge to clean out closets and cupboards, and to dust those corners I have been bypassing all summer.

Most of my flowers have died in the garden but there are still some stalwart blossoms refusing to succumb to the cold frosty air. I love digging in the flower beds and caring for my plants, but by the time fall arrives, I'm ready for a reprieve from battling weeds and bugs. However, by next spring my fingers will be itching to get into the earth and plant a few more varieties of perennials and expand the borders of the beds just a little more.

October 20, 1991

A letter came in the mail from a young man in prison requesting that I visit him. I learned to know him many years ago when he came to our youth group meetings at church where Ike and I had served as advisors.

I had visited at the prison before, but Ike had been with me then. The thought of going alone and being locked up for an hour in the long narrow room filled with prisoners and visitors intimidated me. Nevertheless, I knew I had to go. Praying for courage I moved with the other visitors through security and found a seat along the wall facing the long center benches where the prisoners sit when they enter.

I saw his smiling face as the guard opened the door and the prisoners filed into the room. He was delighted that I had come and talked excitedly as he told me of his conversion and the Bible study group that had formed on his cell block. His love for the Lord was so evident as he went on telling me stories about other inmates which he and his Christian prisoner friends had won for the Lord. He said, "I told my girlfriend that someday I was going back to that little church where I attended youth meetings and when I am released from here, that's what I plan to do." He asked me to pray for his family, especially his mother, who was a bartender; to pray that he'd be able to stay away from the drink that had led to his downfall.

The hour passed quickly and as I left, I thanked the Lord for bringing me there to show me another example of how He works in the lives of His people.

October 27, 1991

In my devotions I was reading about the fruits of the spirit; love, joy, peace, long-suffering, gentleness, goodness, faith, meekness, and temperance.

Joy! Yes, I can truthfully say joy is coming back into my life. It's come slowly, hesitatingly, and sometimes it only stays a short time before slipping out the door again, but it makes its appearance more frequently these days. Each person sees life differently and has different experiences. Each one has to look for joy. How often we are blinded to the things God sends to give us joy. Many times I have dwelt on the negative, refusing to see the good things God has for me. Sorrow and pain are also part of life, but we don't have to remain in their valley. Valleys have hills on either side, hills that must be climbed in order to view the beauty and experience the joy beyond.

November 15, 1991

I noticed a lump in my neck and the doctor ordered an x-ray. The report came back from the hospital that it most likely is malignant. Cancer sounds so ominous and I don't look forward to treatments with all the discomfort I've heard it involves. But I know the Lord won't send more than I can endure.

Perhaps my homecoming is not too far away. It would be wonderful to be in heaven with the Lord.

This morning I read in James 5:11, "Brothers, as an example of patience in the face of suffering, take the prophets who spoke in the name of the Lord. As you know, we consider blessed those who have persevered. You have heard of Job's perseverance and have seen what the Lord finally brought about. The Lord is full of compassion and mercy." He has been compassionate and merciful to me. I know He'll not let me down even if this growth is malignant.

December 4, 1991

I returned from the hospital yesterday, after surgery to remove the growth in my neck and my submandibular gland. (I never realized I had such a thing until now.) The doctors concluded that I didn't have a malignancy after all. There were many people praying for me and I don't know if the hospital's diagnosis was incorrect or if the Lord intervened. Either way, the Lord is the healer and I thank Him for it.

December 11, 1991

It has been two years since Ike's death. How does one know when they have reached the summit of healing when climbing the mountain of grief? I haven't the answer, because just the time you think you have arrived at the top and that healing is complete, the fog clears and you see another peak that must be conquered.

But with time the pain is diminished. We learn to feel comfortable with our new and different lives and fit into a new kind of normality. Maybe when we can truthfully say without reservation, "Thank you, Lord, for this experience," then perhaps healing is complete.

Postscript

In 1992, the "Isaac Martin High School" in Costa Rica was built in memory of Ike. Both Derick and Lisa Matamoras, Betsy's grandchildren, are students at this school.

In 1994, Betsy Martin married Paul Brackbill, the man she alluded to in her journal who played piano and accordion for her music programs at the Mennonite Home. They are retired and live a happy life together near Lancaster, Pennsylvania.

Traveling to visit her four children and seven grandchildren who live in California, Kentucky, Texas, and Costa Rica, has been a great pleasure for them.

They also enjoy volunteering at the Mennonite Home on a regular basis. Paul continues to paint with oils and Betsy loves working in her flower garden.

God has been good and they are grateful for His bringing them together and enriching them with His love.

The men responsible for Ike's death have never been found.